KUNSTHAUS ZÜRICH

David Chipperfield Architects Berlin and the Kunsthaus Zürich

Scheidegger & Spiess

TABLE OF CONTENTS

The extension of the Kunsthaus will open to the public as we tentatively emerge from a period of isolation from each other. Reflecting on the events of the last year and the changes imposed on our way of life, we might seek to understand the lessons this suspension has provided and to anticipate opportunities for change. While much of the speculation is likely exaggerated, it is clear that this moment marks change, both emotional and physical. As architects, we are uncertain about how it will affect our future, but this time has been a rare opportunity to take a more detached view of the present. Over recent years we have increasingly seen our cities shaped by the forces of investment and land value, rather than being formed around our needs and aspirations as citizens. When the idea of the city as something that belongs to and reflects its citizens is abandoned, then so is the vital idea of the city itself lost.

It is inevitable that we question whether the experience of the pandemic will force us to radically alter our cities, the places we work and the spaces where we meet, but perhaps the reality is that we have developed a clearer awareness of the world around us. Under these conditions, the role our built environment plays in giving us both shelter and community is more sharply in focus. We feel the value of the parks in giving us space to move and breathe, as well as the services and technological infrastructure that keep our cities functioning. But we are also more aware that the city and its citizens depend on a social and cultural infrastructure too. These institutions represent not only our desire for knowledge and inspiration, but also give form to common aspirations, our desire to better ourselves individually and collectively.

In this mood of reflection, we can look back over the last thirty years as a period of extraordinary proliferation of new museums and extensions, and a substantial shift in their importance. No longer just repositories of beautiful artefacts, they are places of education, instruction, and dialogue. Museums have tried to broaden their audience, extend their outreach, increase their visitors and expand their cultural and social relevance as a destination. Their offer has become more appealing, not only through an enlargement of galleries but also amenities and activities. As we found other systems to convey information, some thought the functions of these institutions would become unnecessary, but the appreciation of works of art and objects, although often an intimate encounter, remains an experience we like to share with our fellow citizens. In an increasingly digital age, the museum has not lost its importance – it has taken on a greater social role.

It must also be said that for many museums becoming more popular is not only desirable for social relevance but necessary to their financial survival. The appeal for funds is part of a continuous process requiring development of programme, facilities, and physical infrastructure to capture larger local and global audiences.

What role has architecture played in all of this change? There is no doubt physical expansion has been important to new programming and accessibility of institutions. but it has also been co-opted into wider issues of branding and visibility. Aspiring to such a role has been both stimulating and perplexing. There has been a tendency to encourage a more spectacular architecture, confusing the role of the building not only as providing infrastructural improvements for displaying art, but also raising the profile of the institution through its image.

The importance of all cultural institutions depends foremost on the role they play in the surrounding community. Their architecture can reinforce their standing and create an environment that stimulates the relationship between the programme and audience. We should neither overestimate the role of architecture in this participation nor underestimate it. As we move forward, museums must continue to engage seriously with the broader issues of society and environment, as well as managing the balance between local and global audiences. At this moment institutions have an even greater responsibility to provoke ideas and provide space for discussion.

These considerations played a part in the development of Kunsthaus Zürich; however the status of the institution and quality of the collections gave the initial authority to the task, allowing us to consider the role of the new building as an act of consolidation.

There was inevitably sensitivity and concerns about the scale of the project and its physical presence in the city. Fortunately, the alignment of these factors allowed us to concentrate on concerns of substance and intent first rather than distractions about image. We could focus our efforts on resolving design ideas that explored the fundamental concerns of the institution: to showcase the collections to the public; to create a building that is both inviting and stimulating; and to create spaces that will encourage understanding and dialogue and reinforce the museum's presence in the city.

As architects, our first step was to generate an organisational concept for how the museum should present the various collections and activities, and how the visitor should be given a sense of orientation. Museums are an exercise in movement and pause, requiring clear circulation that allows the visitor to wander in a sense of freedom. Our decision was based on a classically inspired enfilade – series of rooms – taking into consideration sequence and orientation, proportion, and lighting, both artificial and natural. The other inspiration was developed from a concern for context. We were conscious of the status of the building in its immediate surroundings, firstly in relation to the original Karl Moser building and the later extensions, and secondly as a contribution to the urban fabric of Zurich. We were extremely aware of the potential impression of the building as an autonomous structure and sought an architectural language consistent to its monumental and civic importance as part of the Kunsthaus on Heimplatz and the redefinition of Heimplatz itself.

Our ambition has been to design a building whose character and personality as an extension are defined by its appropriateness not by its desire for exceptionalism. It purposely avoids the need to gravitate to the superficial gestures of self-referential architecture. While establishing its own identity it looks for what it shares with the place in material and form, inspired by the city around it. Looking at the completed building, I am confident that it contributes not only to the importance of the institution of the Kunsthaus itself and of the role of culture in our shared future, but also as a piece of urban infrastructure giving form to civic aspirations through the representation of its architecture and the new importance of Heimplatz in the public space of Zurich.

David Chipperfield
Founder David Chipperfield Architects
March 2021

A site for active and contemplative experiences

—

Four participants discuss their ideas and the collaborative process that went into creating the new Kunsthaus building.

Sabine von Fischer

HOW WONDERFUL THAT VIDEO TECHNOLOGY HAS ENABLED US TO CONDUCT THIS CONVERSATION ABOUT YOUR COLLABORATION FOR THE NEW KUNST-HAUS ZÜRICH, AND IN SUCH A SPONTANEOUS MANNER. THE RECENT EXTENSION HAS DOUBLED THE SIZE OF THE MUSEUM. CHRISTOPH BECKER, AS DIRECTOR OF KUNSTHAUS ZÜRICH, YOU HAVE COMMENTED ON THIS BY SAYING THAT IT 'HASN'T JUST INCREASED IN SIZE, IT HAS CHANGED ITS CHARACTER'. DO YOU THINK THE PUBLIC IS LIKELY TO UNDERSTAND THAT THE MUSEUM DOESN'T INTEND TO BE AN INSTITUTION DETACHED FROM URBAN LIFE?

Christoph Becker

The Kunsthaus has served as a centre for contemporary art in the middle of the city on Heimplatz since 1910. With its collection, it has developed into a large museum of truly European dimensions. By expanding the building and taking the next step into the 21st century, we are continuing to build on the idea of an open institution. We are creating new spaces for art and the public and thus provide the general public with a new cultural site in the middle of the city.

Sabine von Fischer

ON THE TOPIC OF OPENNESS AND THE PUBLIC, MY NEXT QUESTION IS FOR THE ARCHITECT IN BERLIN: CHRISTOPH FELGER, YOU'VE BEEN WORKING ON DEVELOPING AN OPEN MUSEUM FOR TWELVE YEARS AND HAVE SAID THAT IT WILL ENCOURAGE PEOPLE TO CROSS OVER THE THRESHOLD INTO THE SANCTU-ARY OF ART. SO HOW MIGHT IT BE POSSIBLE FOR ARCHITECTURE TO SIMULTANEOUSLY PROTECT ART AND OPEN ITSELF UP TO THE CITY?

Christoph Felger

Protection is an aspect that today has to be attributed more likely to the astronomically increased prices of works of art and the resulting security requirements. I'm really not sure whether we should even be talking about 'protection' at all within the context of an active or contemplative art experience. If this longing for a space for contemplation can be fulfilled at all, it's actually more a question of controlling visitor numbers. Suppose I'm standing in a tightly packed crowd in front of Leonardo da Vinci's 'Mona Lisa'. In that case, this will undoubtedly be a very different experience of a work of art than when I can experience it with a few people or even alone. I think it is precisely this aspect that reflects a major dilemma that all cultural institutions face today.

Sabine von Fischer

AND YET, DESPITE THIS DILEMMA, YOU'RE LOOKING TO MAKE THE MUSEUM ACCESSIBLE TO AS MANY PEOPLE AS POSSIBLE?

Christoph Felger

Of course, absolutely! We have to change our view of the museum as something exclusive and elitist; fortunately, many museums understood and have been working on this for a while. Though there are still museums that manage to attract less than thirty percent of the local community. I firmly believe that the museum must become a popular institution for all citizens. The International Council of Museums has also agreed on this. Developments such as these are important, and the Tate Modern in London is perhaps the most significant example in Europe of this 'opening up' of the institution. What remains important here is striking a balance between the number of visitors, which is necessary for the public and the economic viability of such buildings, and the protection of contemplative spaces that also enable the individual experience of art. In the new extension, the publicly accessible hall in particular, which spans the entire building and aims to arouse interest and curiosity among passers-by, is an invitation to the population of Zurich. Perhaps it is the most essential architectural element that we have given to Zurich in the context of this idea of opening up.

Christoph Becker
Director of Kunsthaus Zürich
—

David Chipperfield
Founder David Chipperfield Architects
(with simultaneous translation)
—

Christoph Felger
Partner and Design Director, David Chipperfield Architects Berlin
—

Wiebke Rösler Häfliger
Director of the City of Zurich's Building Surveyor's Office,
Chair of the Building Committee
—

Moderator:
Sabine von Fischer
Architectural Editor

'The building stands there and adds new dimensions to the square – you can already feel them.'

Sabine von Fischer
DAVID CHIPPERFIELD, YOU MENTIONED THE TATE MODERN IN LONDON, THE CITY WHERE YOU ALSO LIVE AND WORK, AS A POINT OF REFERENCE. THE TURBINE HALL IS LARGER THAN THE HALL IN ZURICH, BUT THE HALL IN ZURICH IS LOCATED IN THE MIDDLE OF THE CITY. IS IT REALLY POSSIBLE TO COMPARE THESE TWO SPACES?

David Chipperfield
We should be careful not to wear out this analogy with the Tate Modern. You don't need to purchase a ticket to enter the large hall at Kunsthaus Zürich, which is also the case with the Tate. The comparison is aimed at the social dimension of the project far more than the spatial dimension, so it makes more sense to approach the topic by way of the altered role of museums. Of course, museums need to preserve and safeguard their treasures, but they should also appeal to broader, less specialised sections of society. Museums are becoming a source of reflection and criticism and, whether they like it or not, are becoming increasingly important for society, at a time when other forms of media such as newspapers are losing the trust of the general public. So, in a sense, the museum is coming to represent or embody a locus of truth and a repository of collective contemplation, thereby becoming part of a cultural and social infrastructure.

Sabine von Fischer
HOW DOES THE MUSEUM'S SOCIAL DIMENSION MANIFEST ITSELF?

David Chipperfield
When Nick Serota, who was the director of the Tate at the time, was asked why he wanted to embark on another building extension, he replied: 'It's become a place to go'; the site had become a destination in its own right. That's what interests us – the fact that, historically speaking, the museum used to be a specific destination that people would go to because they wanted to see a particular exhibition, perhaps Cézanne. But these days, the Tate is a place that people visit just for the sake of it. One day, people in Zurich might also say, 'Let's go to the Kunsthaus', without knowing what

13

is currently being exhibited. Museums are becoming increasingly important, and artists are increasingly addressing key contemporary issues, which means that the museum is increasingly becoming a forum for social debate. We wanted to put a large, open space in the centre of the extension, like they have at the Tate, enabling visitors to orient themselves in the building and mediate between the two separate realms of the public and the institution.

Sabine von Fischer
SO, THE HALL AS A PUBLIC SPACE IN A PRIVATE BUILDING IS LIKELY TO REMAIN A SITE OF NEGOTIATION AND DIALOGUE IN THE FUTURE. WIEBKE RÖSLER, WHAT ARE YOUR HOPES FOR WHAT WILL HAPPEN IN THERE?

Wiebke Rösler Häfliger
The large hall was at the centre of the architectural design from the very beginning. One very important reason why this project won the competition was the hall and how it connected everything together: the hall connects Heimplatz with the garden and the university district. You asked me what my hopes are: I would like people to use the space and pass through the hall on their way to other neighbourhood parts. Perhaps they will end up staying for a moment and soaking in the space in all its magnificence. The hall invites us to take a moment to stop and discover. People will experience the site through the architecture and space it offers without much in the way of an explanation.

David Chipperfield
It's important to understand that architecture does not prescribe a particular kind of behaviour. For a long time, we've advocated the idea that buildings should not be functionally determined; this is an important aspect of our work. But what architecture is capable of doing is provoking, suggesting, encouraging certain behaviours. Kunsthaus Zürich is essentially a conservative piece of architecture based on well-established principles of museum construction: it has rooms, enfilades, a point of orientation. When you arrive, you want to find out where the building goes and how big

it is; you essentially desire to get lost and find your bearings. That's why the hall is so important: it serves as the key to the building; it acts as a mediator between the city's openness, the seclusion of the building while also guiding the visitors. The hall is the connective element. As Christoph Felger already mentioned, architecture determines the framework in which something can occur rather than the content. It suggests the potential happenings within the space by rousing our imagination for a number of different possibilities, rather than just one.

Christoph Becker
As simple as the whole thing may seem now, it was actually a rather difficult task. For one thing, the hall had to provide a connection point to the university district, as well as – this was our hope from the outset – illustrate what the institution has to offer: a bar, a shop, an art education centre with large rooms, a ballroom, and a broad staircase leading to the first floor, which is where the rooms displaying the artworks begin. The hall, which people often describe as forming an axis of sorts, is ultimately a space you enter and decide which direction to take. The idea is not for people to simply walk through the space and out the other side without purchasing a ticket. When you are in the space and look left, right, or above you, you will see that the museum reveals itself in all its high architectural complexity and that it continues into the spaces behind, beside, and above the hall.

Christoph Felger
The hall extends all the way from the facade facing Heimplatz to the garden and from the floor to the roof. Upstairs there are the enfilades that David has already described. The architecture creates a framework within which I can move from active to passive sensations in a series of very different kinds of spaces – from the open hall to very small cabinet-like exhibition spaces, some of which are lit from the side or above to generate a sense of intimacy. The route through the museum leads you through different atmospheres and environments that enable both active and contemplative experiences of art.

Sabine von Fischer

WHAT DOES THE EXTERIOR SPACE GAIN FROM THE ADDITION OF THESE NEW INTERIOR SPACES?

Wiebke Rösler Häfliger

The sheer size and capacity of the Chipperfield building have caused the urban exterior space, specifically Heimplatz, to become more significant than ever before. The building dimensions are good for the square, and I think it directly affects people when they walk across Heimplatz. The garden has added another outside space, which is also sure to be well received by the public.

Christoph Felger

In this sense, the hall can be seen as an extension of the public space outside since it brings the city closer to the people and closer to art. I hope that the citizens of Zurich will understand and accept the hall as such a spatial connecting element and also come to regard it as their own.

David Chipperfield

But it will never be a truly public space, even if perceived that way. Like the main hall of a post office or the main concourse of a railway station, the hall belongs to an institution and seeks to be part of the community.

Wiebke Rösler Häfliger

You only have to find the courage to step into the hall through this golden door!

Sabine von Fischer

SO, YOU HAVE TO HAVE THE COURAGE TO ENTER THE HALL, AS WIEBKE RÖSLER SAYS. BUT IT'S ALSO A SITE OF INFINITE POSSIBILITIES, AS CHRISTOPH BECKER AND CHRISTOPH FELGER JUST EXPLAINED. DAVID CHIPPERFIELD SAID THAT THESE DAYS ART IS ALLOWED TO DO THINGS THAT NOBODY ELSE HAS THE LIBERTY OF DOING – NOT EVEN THE NEWS-PAPERS – WHICH IS WHY WE'LL PROBABLY CONTINUE TO KEEP AN EYE ON WHAT'S ALLOWED TO HAPPEN IN THIS HALL.

Wiebke Rösler Häfliger

Like skateboarding, for example? Ultimately it is conceivable that any outside activity could also take place inside the hall; the only difference is that we are in a covered area in close proximity to other people who are using the space.

David Chipperfield

But you also have to keep in mind that even the outdoor spaces in Zurich are kept incredibly tidy! (laughs) And, of course, the space is monitored; there are staff members here.

Christoph Becker

To be sure, we have allowed people to ride skateboards in the big exhibition hall before, and it worked well, apart from the noise. A lot can happen in the hall; it's actually designed to be multifunctional. As for the building's architectural design, one of the most important considerations was to ensure that the hall serves not as an exit route but as a place to hold events involving a great number of people – whether they be arts-related events, hiring out the space for private events, or our own events like parties and balls, which we are now able to offer thanks to the ball-room. This means the hall is as much a social space as it is a cultural site. A defining characteristic of the 21st-century museum is that the space does not simply facilitate an 'elitist enjoyment of art', but rather that it helps culture find its way into the public sphere.

Sabine von Fischer

IN RECENT MONTHS, THE PUBLIC HAS BEEN PARTICU-LARLY INTERESTED IN THE BÜHRLE COLLECTION, WHICH IS HOUSED IN THE NEW BUILDING, AND ITS CONTROVERSIAL HISTORY CONCERNING ARMS PRODUCTION DURING WORLD WAR II. WHAT WOULD HAPPEN IF A SPONTANEOUS DISCUSSION FORUM ON THIS TOPIC WERE TO TAKE PLACE IN THE HALL?

Christoph Becker

The hall would easily withstand it. From the very beginning, we expected – and hoped – that discussions would occur, not only regarding this very significant and striking expansion of the institution but also its contents. Of course, we're keen to provide more space for our own collection and present it differently from how it has been displayed for the past one hundred years. We also want to show that there's a desire for large private collections in Zurich and Switzerland to be close to public institutions. Discussions will inevitably arise for some of the collections since they were created in the 20th century. From the very beginning, the design concept for the Bührle Collection took into consideration the fact that housing it in the Kunsthaus extension would attract a different kind of public than the collection did during the first fifty or sixty years of its existence when it was situated on Zollikerstrasse in a private mansion. The collection is of art-historical significance and has a controversial historical background, which we also plan to delineate in the new building. I think that contemporary museums are responsible not only for offering visitors a 'pure enjoyment of art', but also for revealing historical contexts and relations, including the social context.

Sabine von Fischer
IN THE NEW KUNSTHAUS BUILDING, OPEN DEBATE AND CONTEMPLATIVE ENJOYMENT OF ART GO HAND IN HAND. IN A FEAT OF TECHNICAL INGENUITY, YOU'VE FOUND A WAY TO MAKE THE BARRIERS BETWEEN THE HALL AND THE EXHIBITION SPACES INVISIBLE: ENTIRE WALLS DISAPPEAR INTO THE FLOOR OR CAN BE PUSHED TO THE SIDE, WHICH ALLOWS PEOPLE TO FULLY EXPERIENCE THE CONNECTIVE CAPACITY OF THE HALL, TO MOVE THROUGH THE BUILDING. FROM A CURATORIAL PERSPECTIVE, IS IT CONCEIVABLE THAT THE ARCHITECTURE'S DYNAMIC SPIRIT MIGHT ALSO SET THE COLLECTIONS IN MOTION?

Christoph Becker
Some collections are intended for private display because this is the manner that best demonstrates what the collection actually is. I think this makes sense in terms of ensuring that the historical background of the collection's creation remains visible. There was never any doubt in our minds that the artworks from the Bührle Collection would initially be shown together, and

that these would also share an affiliation of sorts with the artworks that were entrusted to the Zürcher Kunstgesellschaft many years ago, which would visualise a continuum of particular works and groups. In a number of cases, changes and slight adjustments are already being made on the edges of some of these compilations that are being moved into the museums. There will also be stark contrasts.

Sabine von Fischer
WHAT KIND OF CONTRAST DO YOU HAVE IN MIND?

Christoph Becker
It's part of the new layout – that visitors don't just chronologically move through art history, but rather that artworks can extend across epochs and styles and enter into dialogue with each other. The concept of the initial layout for the new Kunsthaus, in both the original building and the extension, is that the works correspond with one another across the epochs.

Christoph Felger
In the context of the discussion about the Bührle Collection, which is currently taking place in the media, I find it interesting that museums may become places of truth. When conventional institutions in politics, religion and the press are losing the public's trust, perhaps the issues and topics fundamental to our societies will start being discussed in buildings such as these. I also believe that museums are increasingly operating as places of negotiation and dialogue. What kind of society do we want to be? What types of values do we want to live by? If the hall can act as a symbol for debating these values, this means we've managed to contribute a great deal – by way of the architecture – to make the new extension a vibrant, lively, social space.

David Chipperfield
From an architectural perspective, the question also arises about the museum's status and significance in society. The museum as an institution has become tremendously important in the past twenty years. It's all about the capacity and willingness to take responsibility. At the same time, it's interesting to see the kinds

of contributions that museums make to the community, while all around us so much is subject to purely private interests. In a social context, the hope is that the museum will be able to make a real contribution to the city's fabric – something that has now become such a rare occurrence in the world of architecture. The museum is becoming a special place – a site for freedom of thought, not just in intellectual terms but also within the urban context.

Sabine von Fischer
THIS FREEDOM WOULD APPLY TO ART AND THE PUBLIC, BUT WHAT ABOUT THE FREEDOM FOR THE ARCHITECTS?

David Chipperfield
For us, designing a museum is a wonderful challenge because it's imbued with so many hopes regarding the kind of impact the architecture will have. The museum is a temple of sorts, a site for independent reflection, and at the same time an opportunity for architecture to also play a social role by contributing something to the community. As architects, we often find ourselves in a situation where we attempt to convince other people of something but don't succeed. Nobody wants to be in that position because ultimately we aspire to promote an idea for the public interest; we have always endeavoured to eschew artistic egotism favouring using our creativity to realise a common idea. Throughout the entirety of the architectural process, Christoph Felger and I always ask ourselves who our client is; is it the people who, for some reason, wish to see an idea realised and then remunerate us for our work? Or is it the general public who will have to put up with the building in the future? In this way, we see the work we do towards realising this common idea as being commissioned by the client and the public.

Sabine von Fischer
THIS MEANS THIS COMMON IDEA ALSO EXTENDS BEYOND THE BUILDING AND IMPACTS THE ENTIRE CITY. YOU'VE BUILT BUILDINGS IN MANY DIFFERENT PARTS OF THE WORLD. WHAT DID YOU MAKE OF YOUR EXPERIENCE IN ZURICH?

David Chipperfield
The cultural terrain that forms the foundation of museums certainly has a significant influence on understanding the concepts of openness and the public sphere. Erecting a building such as this for the public at Heimplatz in Zurich is an entirely different experience than it would be if we were to do so in Mexico City. We've built in a number of places where only the rudiments of a public sphere exist. But I really ought to stress once again that this does not apply to Zurich! The sense of community in Switzerland and its concomitant social ideas and procedures are well-established. Of course, this isn't always the case; we've been in so many places where the public structures have been entirely eroded.

Sabine von Fischer
THAT WAS A REAL SHOWER OF PRAISE FOR THE CITY OF ZURICH. WIEBKE RÖSLER, WHAT CHALLENGES DID YOU FACE?

Wiebke Rösler Häfliger
As is the case with every project, our first task is to convince the politicians. We have to know that the various political authorities are on our side, and ultimately also the electorate. Some individual associations and neighbourhood members made life difficult for us by bringing about delays to the construction process. To be more specific, there were objections, but there are always objections, especially in Switzerland, where the population is allowed to have a say. That is why the construction and the opening were delayed.

Sabine von Fischer
BENEDIKT LODERER HAS DOCUMENTED ALL THE CONTENTION SURROUNDING THE VARIOUS OBJECTIONS IN THE FIRST VOLUME OF THIS BOOK SERIES, SO WE DON'T NEED TO GO INTO IT AGAIN HERE.

Wiebke Rösler Häfliger
The fact that it was jointly supported by private patrons and the public definitely helped the project succeed. Overall, I'd say that the process has gone really well since the competition took place twelve years ago.

'For us, designing a museum is a wonderful challenge because it's imbued with so many hopes regarding the kind of impact the architecture will have.'

'One day, people in Zurich might also say, "Let's go to the Kunsthaus", without knowing what is currently being exhibited.'

Sabine von Fischer
A FEW ADJUSTMENTS WERE MADE IN TERMS OF THE SIZE OF THE BUILDING. WOULD YOU SAY IT'S NOW TOO BIG?

Wiebke Rösler Häfliger
During the project development phase, we did something positive about urban development – both for the courtyard and for Heimplatz as a whole – by slightly reducing and shifting the entire volume of the building. And of course, this also reduced the costs. We collaborated with the architect to develop this new building, and as always our concerns were quality, time, and cost; these are the three factors we always keep in mind when representing our clients. It was an ongoing negotiation. I'm extremely happy that we could work on this development together and that the building has ended up the way it has – only not quite as large as we had initially planned. But now I think its dimensions are just right.

Christoph Becker
We formulated the programme for the building extension very precisely and allowed for the space that would be needed for the art and public of the 21st century. These adjustments, as you call them, were made almost exclusively in areas that have no bearing on the internal workings of the museum – like the car park, for example. But we didn't increase the size and capacity of the building just for the sake of making it bigger, but rather to alter the character of the museum: doubling the size of the building does not mean that the exhibition space has been doubled; instead, our main priority was to increase the amount of space available to the public, which in turn changes the character of the Kunsthaus as a whole, because overall it allows us to offer more spaces, and more generous spaces, including for art education and in terms of hiring out the rooms, some of which can be used by the public.

David Chipperfield
The question of size is relatively complicated: is this extension happening for the institution to display more

artworks and increase admissions? Or is the museum striving to establish a greater presence in the city? Sometimes these things work together, and sometimes they obstruct one another; museum directors are under incredible pressure.

Christoph Felger

From the beginning, we were aware that the size, extent, and importance of the extension might put the existing Kunsthaus in the shade and minimise its significance. I think we understood that very quickly, and it was one of the main points of dispute in the initial stage of the competition: how could we generate a sense of autonomy on the other side of Heimplatz – because the building's location necessitates this autonomy – while simultaneously fostering a connection to and an appreciation of what already exists? We still advocate our solution of a simple, clear, and strong building structure. Ultimately the adjustments, which constituted roughly ten percent of the total volume of our initial building proposal, were marginal. But they were undoubtedly part of the atmosphere of negotiation and dialogue that will hopefully continue to shape the life and identity of this building in the future.

David Chipperfield

I'd like to second that; the adjustments did not cause any substantial changes to the building. But it was necessary to have this discussion to ensure that everyone concerned about the size of the building had their voice heard. There were two main points of criticism regarding our project: that it was too big and too boring. We had to take this discussion seriously because, ultimately, we had no indication of how the building would end up coming across when we were designing it. I was always convinced that the size was not the point. The building forms the missing fourth side to a public square and contributes to urban development. The objective is to ensure that Heimplatz becomes part of the urban space; the architectural contribution is a secondary concern. But the other accusation – that the building design was boring – weighed more heavily on our minds, especially if the extension were to end up being bigger than the building that was being extended. It was very important

'The museum is becoming a special place – a site for freedom of thought, not just in intellectual terms but also within the urban context.'

19

to us that the extension maintains a sense of respect for the original building.

Christoph Felger
We've often referred to this project metaphorically as a 'family', in which, in our case, the child was bigger than its mother from birth. This child certainly belongs to a new generation. The gesture of openness was important to us: to get into the Moser building, which appears relatively closed from the outside, you first have to venture through a narrow entrance gate. Only in the foyer, you realise that the sacred halls of art are anything but inaccessible; inside, they are open and flooded with light. With the extension, we aimed to transport these interior experiences to the outside and ensure the smoothest possible transition from the outside to the inside by means of this gesture of opening – the hall with its large windows.

David Chipperfield
But this doesn't necessarily have to mean erecting a conspicuous or self-referential building. We wanted to express a sense of respect towards Karl Moser's original building on the opposite side of the square and for the entire complex of the various Kunsthaus buildings. So the size is determined by the urban planning, and the architectural character is determined by the building opposite. The extension seeks to boldly integrate itself into the whole. It should look so self-assured, so confident, that it's able to demand people's trust and adopt a mediating role.

Christoph Felger
It's a question of trust within the context of the city as a whole. The jury report at the time expressed concerns that the building might end up not only looking too boring but also seemingly too historical with the natural stone facade.

David Chipperfield
With regard to the question of confidence, I have a comment for our Swiss colleagues in particular: the loss of confidence in architecture is also linked to the demise of manual skills. The visual effect often has to compensate for the physical substance because

the construction quality is so poor in so many places. We've benefitted greatly from the fact that such a high level of quality has been upheld throughout this process. In many of the locations where we build, the holy trinity of quality, time, and cost is levelled off, and quality ends up losing out; then it becomes solely about money and time. We may not always have been certain, but now, in retrospect, we can confidently say that the decision to maintain a high level of quality has paid off and that it was even possible to create a supposedly 'boring' building under these conditions.

Wiebke Rösler Häfliger
(laughs) That's really exciting. It's exactly like David said. I do not think the building is boring, and naturally, I feel a sense of pride that we managed to work together with the owners to achieve this level of quality. They were a pillar we could lean on. When it comes to the triangle of construction management, there will always be one element that you have to be flexible about, and that was where we were flexible.

Sabine von Fischer
MOST PEOPLE SEEM TO ADJUST RELATIVELY QUICKLY TO THE SIZE, BUT IT MIGHT TAKE A LITTLE LONGER WHEN IT COMES TO THE BOREDOM ASPECT. YOU'VE ULTIMATELY CREATED SOMETHING PARADOXICAL WITH THE FACADE'S EXPRESSION: THE BUILDING LOOKS SIMULTANEOUSLY LIKE A COLOSSUS AND, BY DISSOLVING INTO A VERTICAL FLOW, A GRACEFUL BUILDING THAT IS REMINISCENT OF THE DIAPHANOUS ARCHITECTURE OF THE GOTHIC PERIOD. HOW DID YOU ACHIEVE THAT?

Christoph Felger
The idea of cladding the building with natural stone arose from contemplating the city. Several important public buildings in Zurich from previous eras have high-quality natural stone facades. We wanted to include the new extension into this canon because we recognised Zurich's architectural heritage in it. We left the stone with a rough-cut finish and rounded the pilaster strips vertically to make this large building tangible. There was a lengthy consultation process to convince the various stakeholders involved. Initially,

a number of them were worried about the sense of heaviness this monolith might impart, but today, many people are actually surprised by its lightness.

Sabine von Fischer
WE BEGAN THIS CONVERSATION BY ADDRESSING THE TOPIC OF THE SPATIAL DUALITY OF SHELTERING AND OPENING. AND WHEN IT CAME TO THE FACADE, YOU WORKED WITH A DUALITY OF HEAVINESS AND LIGHTNESS. HOW WERE YOU ABLE TO CONVINCE THE OTHER PARTIES INVOLVED OF SUCH AN ABSTRACT IDEA?

Christoph Felger
What we presented in the competition was first and foremost a promise. Our experience has taught us to ensure that this process of dialogue and negotiation be open and transparent from the outset. After all, we're demanding an enormous amount of trust from the client and from everyone else involved in the project. In Zurich, we were met with open ears; this was my experience when dealing with representatives of both the city and the arts community. From the very beginning, there was a transparent and familiar atmosphere in which we could talk about everything thoroughly and honestly; we were in constant negotiation with each other, also in the context of this triangle of time, cost, and quality. In this process, the 1:1 scale facade mock-up was incredibly helpful; we tried many different ideas on it to ultimately be able to make collective decisions. I think that it is often underestimated how important the quality of the culture of cooperation and dialogue is in such a process for the final quality of the building.

David Chipperfield
In a sense, we were also protected by the professionalism with which the competition was conducted, and with which the city later organised the development of the building project. This also applies to how we handled criticism and objections. The professional commitment of both the City of Zurich and the Kunsthaus was vital for the project. We have also had experiences in the past where everyone just drops everything at the first sign of a problem.

Our experiences in Berlin led us to become accustomed to communicating our ideas in an atmosphere of scepticism, and it's also not a bad thing when architects are required to explain themselves. The best and most successful projects emerge from the processes that are conducted in a spirit of cooperation. It can be productive to sit in a circle and have the sense that everybody around you is on your side. We had the great fortune of being surrounded by people who were also keen to progress the project. This made the whole experience not only successful but also pleasant.

Christoph Becker
That makes it sound like it was all smooth and straightforward, but in Switzerland, quality can also come under pressure when compromises need to be made. We wanted the design by David Chipperfield Architects to be realised, because it was the option that promised to best reflect the contents of the museum. We could imagine making a compromise or two in certain places, but not in very many places. There was also a small group of people who seemed to only be interested in compromise. But I actually found it incredibly heartening to have a high consistency of opinions throughout almost the entire process, when it came to talking about the feasibility and the actual realisation of the project, from the big picture to the minutest details. We were incredibly fortunate in this sense with the Kunsthaus project, and we should not take that for granted.

Wiebke Rösler Häfliger
The quality that's exhibited in the architectural design constitutes the core of our work. We are proud to facilitate architectural designs and good architecture. As the client representative for the City of Zurich, a cornerstone of what we do is seeking to realise good architectural designs, and in this case, it's turned out well. I'm really pleased; it's beautiful.

Sabine von Fischer
AND FOLLOWING THAT FAVOURABLE ACCOUNT OF THE PROJECT, LET'S NOW LOOK TOWARDS THE FUTURE: THERE'S A VAGUE POSSIBILITY THAT

THE NEWLY INSTALLED WHITE MARBLE USED IN THE EXTENSION WILL NO LONGER ABRUPTLY COLLIDE WITH THE PROVISIONAL ASPHALT SURFACE. THE COMPETITION ALSO WELCOMED IDEAS FOR REDEVELOPING THE SPACE OF HEIMPLATZ BETWEEN THE ORIGINAL BUILDING AND THE EXTENSION. THE PEOPLE AT DAVID CHIPPERFIELD ARCHITECTS WERE QUITE DARING AND SOUGHT TO MAKE THE CONNECTION BETWEEN THE TWO BUILDINGS VISIBLE ABOVEGROUND IN THE SQUARE, INSTEAD OF JUST BEING UNDERGROUND: THEIR PLAN WAS TO LAY LIGHT-COLOURED MARBLE ALL THE WAY ACROSS HEIMPLATZ, FROM THE FLOOR OF ONE ENTRANCE HALL TO THE FLOOR OF THE LARGE HALL, BUT THE IDEA WAS REJECTED. I'D NOW LIKE TO POSE THE SAME QUESTION ONCE AGAIN TO WIEBKE RÖSLER: IS THERE ANY CHANCE THAT THIS IDEA MIGHT BE RECONSIDERED IN THE FUTURE?

Wiebke Rösler Häfliger
The redevelopment of Heimplatz is an incredibly complex and politically charged issue that does not fall within my remit. The planning authority is in charge of this project. Actually, the Heimplatz redevelopment project should have been completed more or less at the same time as or even before the Kunsthaus was renovated, but that wasn't possible for political reasons. The square experiences a huge pressure of use, also in terms of the volume of traffic. Marble is an obvious choice because it's been part of the flooring in front of the Kunsthaus for decades. It's protected, and it should be continued in one way or another. Heimplatz has been provisionally refurbished with asphalt to the extent that people can now use the square. The use of marble has been considered, and we know that it will stay, but only in certain sections of the square. For example, marble can't be laid where the road is and where the lorries drive, but new marble flooring will certainly be installed in other parts of the square. We're also looking forward to the refurbishment of the existing marble on Heimplatz.

David Chipperfield
I have to say I'm not at all concerned about the fact that Heimplatz is not yet finished. It's pretty standard for the surrounding area not to be finished when a building is completed. What's most important is ensuring that Heimplatz becomes a city square and belongs to the city. It should be influenced by the surrounding buildings but not overdetermined by them. Cities develop over time. Now that the Kunsthaus extension has been completed, attention is shifting to the exterior space. The new situation also sheds new light on the design of the square, and thus also on managing the traffic that passes through it. It wouldn't be desirable to have complete continuity between the Kunsthaus buildings on both sides of the square. Still, the design of the public space at Heimplatz definitely requires the utmost attention.

Sabine von Fischer
SO WE'LL BE WAITING A WHILE FOR THE NEW SQUARE. BUT WHEN WILL WE SEE IF THE CONCEPT OF THIS BUILDING – ITS OPENNESS AND INTERNAL DYNAMISM – IS ACCEPTED BY THE GENERAL PUBLIC?

Wiebke Rösler Häfliger
I would say: straight away! The building stands there and adds new dimensions to the square – you can already feel them. Pipilotti Rist's 'Tastende Lichter' plays on the facades of the buildings. I'm confident that people will use this outside space even before the opening takes place in autumn and benefit from the new situation. The structure defines this square and the surrounding urban space with a great sense of naturalness.

Christoph Becker
The urban environment has certainly changed in recent months. Rämistrasse and the area surrounding the Kunsthaus have recorded an influx of galleries, extending into the historic city centre, and a gastronomic upgrade is planned through the Kunsthaus Bar, as well as culinary initiatives aimed at channelling the influx of people into this new location. In fact, this has already begun. A new cultural centre is emerging here, which the Schauspielhaus definitely also contributes to. The garden was also an essential component of our concept. Accessing culture and entering buildings dedicated to culture play a different role today than they did ten

or fifteen years ago. Members of the general public don't just perceive and appreciate the interior of cultural institutions, but also the exterior, the surroundings. In this respect, the garden performs an important function for the building as a whole. David has designed his own garden architecture – known as Rondell – which has now been implemented.

Sabine von Fischer
DAVID CHIPPERFIELD, YOU'VE BUILT MUSEUMS WORLDWIDE AND HAVE ALSO WITNESSED THEIR EVOLUTION OVER TIME. WHAT ARE YOUR HOPES FOR THE FUTURE OF THE KUNSTHAUS AT HEIMPLATZ?

David Chipperfield
We architects take a step back when a building is being constructed. Once it's completed, it's no longer our project, and other people take over. Our task is simply to set the priorities in the right order. Architecture should never become too overbearing; for example, it should never compete with the art. But it needs to be powerful enough that it enhances our experience of art. Achieving this balance is not easy, but we must pursue. In around 1980, when many museums were being built according to extravagant architectural designs, the renowned art critic David Sylvester stated: 'Art has no greater enemy than the architect.' This was a reaction to a time when architects were channelling their creative energy in the wrong direction. We're continually asked to design museums because we strive to strike a balance between architectural integrity and the infrastructure of the spaces, the orientation, and all of these things that also have a lot to do with perception. I'm confident that this building is a robust piece of museum infrastructure that will be used intelligently by the current and future directors and curators.

Sabine von Fischer
CHRISTOPH FELGER, AFTER TWELVE YEARS OF INTENSIVE WORK, YOU WERE UNABLE TO ATTEND THE OPENING BECAUSE OF THE PANDEMIC AND HAVE NOT YET BEEN ABLE TO WITNESS THE FINISHED BUILDING IN PERSON. WHAT KIND OF EXPERIENCE DO YOU HAVE IN MIND?

Christoph Felger
As David puts it, life and art should be the focus now, not the building. For this reason, I would like architecture to be perceived as embodying a kind of 'meaningful casualness' in the end. I was pleased that friends from Zurich kept telling me over the past year how they now experience the new extension as a natural part of the city when they go past by tram or by foot.

Sabine von Fischer
I HOPE THAT YOU – AND ALL OF US – WILL SOON BE ABLE TO TRAVEL AGAIN AND EXPERIENCE THE SPACES IN PERSON. THANK YOU VERY MUCH FOR THIS STIMULATING CONVERSATION.

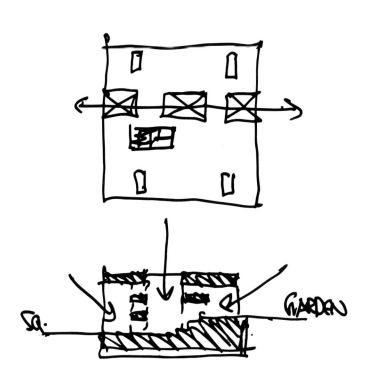

ristoph Felger
sponsible Partner
d Design Director
David Chipperfield
chitects Berlin

The design for the extension of the Kunsthaus Zürich follows our conviction that every new building should primarily be a building of its place and its culture as well as its social and physical environment – a local building.

Due to our culturally shaped perception, we associate formal features such as street, alley, square, and block with the idea of the familiar city. But there are other factors, too, that determine the way we think about the quality of our cities, such as typological hierarchy, structural compactness, functional diversity, social density, and how the cityscape is maintained. A thoughtful engagement with criteria such as scale, form, and materiality can help us steer a symbiosis of urban planning and architecture and their effect on us humans. In the best-case scenario, we can design them so that the spaces and places we create have a positive influence on us and our well-being.

In a city like Zurich, maintaining a balance between the aspects mentioned above has always generated security, comfort, and belonging. We associate them with the values of an enlightened civil society, which shape our ideas of progress, self-determination, and participation to this day.

At the same time, the architecture in Zurich, like that of many cities which have grown continuously and never been destroyed, is always building upon something that already exists. No architecture ever stands autonomously, simply detached from its context. For this reason, the architecture in Zurich is therefore always a component of an already existing entity and thus of memories and feelings about 'existing places' and their timeless significance for their residents. Sensing and understanding the site-specific characteristics of the building site on Heimplatz in this context provides a creative foundation for our exploration with urban planning and architectural ideas. They determine our strategies for the design of the extension for the Kunsthaus Zürich.

As a city in a constant state of growth, Zurich radiates a very particular blend of urban tranquillity and prudence, which seems to rest upon a forward-looking understanding of 'change through continuity' or, conversely, of 'continuity through change'. As architects, we have been following the increasingly intensifying sense of global competitiveness between cities for years. Zurich has responded to this with unmistakable urban gravity that lends the city its unique character. Neither urban exuberance nor architectural hubris are necessary or appropriate in Zurich. Instead, it seems as if an unwritten law sets the city's structural mass into a careful and well-balanced relationship to the local conditions and needs of its residents. Within this condition public architecture seems to have developed the status of a 'meaningful casualness'. Against this background, every architectural intervention on Heimplatz has to deal with and position itself, with this overarching urban self-image of a 'city at rest'.

The brief of the competition asked to more than double the area of the existing Kunsthaus Zürich, making it the largest art museum in Switzerland. The new building would accommodate the collections of classical modernism, the Emil Bührle Collection, temporary exhibitions and art from 1960 onwards and connect it spatially and functionally to the existing Kunsthaus via a visitor passage running beneath Heimplatz.

With these objectives in mind, we were aware from the start that the new extension could overshadow the existing cultural buildings on Heimplatz, the Kunst- and Schauspielhaus, in terms of size, extent and importance. Ultimately, we were concerned with an urban and architectural balancing act in which the new extension was to be given due independence a building of its size deserves, while at the same time allowing the new house to relate to the existing buildings in a unifying and appreciative manner.

In the context of our overriding understanding of the city as a 'dormant unit in change through continuity', we opted for an approach of 'unexcited expansion' through the inclusion and further development of site-specific features and principles. Under this premise, with the extension to the Kunsthaus Zürich we wanted to create a natural place for encounters, lingering, and contemplation in, for and from Zurich.

Our design provides a spatial counterpoint to the busy, noisy, hectic traffic intersection at Heimplatz, offering an inviting and peaceful place for social interaction, as well as a place to enjoy art. In addition, the specificity of the building is intended to bring the previously undefined Heimplatz closer to a state of urban completeness. Due to the strongly diverging architectures and the high volume of traffic on Heimplatz, we decided to place a contemplative, horizontal structure at the square's northern edge with sufficient distance from the traffic.

In terms of 'change through continuity', the architectural appearance of the extension is based on the example of surrounding traditional natural stone facades, as can be found on the existing Kunsthaus by Karl Moser and in a number of other important public buildings in Zurich. Such buildings represent Zurich's architectural history and the aesthetic influence of an enlightened civil society, which our extension intends to reflect. With its slender and regularly arranged pilaster strips and sawn surfaces made of Jura limestone from Liesberg, the extension combines traditional and innovative craftsmanship. It thus embeds the building in its architectural context in a contemporary manner.

Regarding the size and location and associated significance in the entire ensemble of Kunsthaus buildings, we wanted the new building's simple and clear form to create a place of orientation between Heimplatz in the south and a newly created garden in the north. At the same time, following our conviction that art should always be exhibited in daylight, the new extension embeds the art experience in an atmosphere of the greatest possible naturalness and familiarity with direct visual connections to the immediate neighbourhood.

In the interplay of building volume and setting, the new extension becomes a resting cube as the urban 'backbone' of Heimplatz. Due to its formal restraint, the new building mediates between all existing and divergent building structures and unites them to form a superordinate urban ensemble – the Heimplatz, which is now enclosed on all four sides. As a 'gateway to the arts', the new Heimplatz also functions as an urban starting point for the 'university mile' of the nearby university campus situated to the north, and the historic old town to the south. In this function, it transforms the location at Heimplatz into a new 'place to pause', a new important socio-urban link between two very different parts of the city beyond the traffic junction.

The building site is located on the former site of the Alte Kantonsschule, which included a natural public pathway that served as a pedestrian shortcut up to the hill or down to the lake, avoiding the adjacent road traffic. In this respect, we were intrigued by the idea of incorporating this already inherent 'public feature' in the location for the new extension. The spacious entrance hall, which spans the entire building from north to south, with its floor-to-ceiling windows that can be read from the outside, is based on this path relationship, which has by now perhaps been forgotten. Via the large windows the entrance hall connects the garden with Heimplatz and thus the building with the city. From here, all uses of the house, whether art education, ballroom, museum shop, bar and thirty-three exhibition halls of different sizes on two upper floors can be reached. The entrance hall, with its diverse views in and out, is the essential connecting spatial element within the building and can be accessed and experienced by visitors even without purchasing a museum ticket. For this very reason, and because all functions are brought together in it, the entrance hall can be described as the architectural heart of the new building. The manifold ways in which the entrance hall can be used will make a significant contribution to the public perception of the Kunsthaus Zürich as a lively cultural venue.

The building's interior organisation is guided by the concept of a 'house of rooms' in which no two rooms are of the same size. The rhythm and sequence of exhibition rooms of different sizes create a lively spatial experience during the exhibition tour, in which the art experience and not the architecture is the focus. This is why we have opted for a restrained materiality, which gives priority to a maximum and varied amount of daylight by way of side-light on the first floor, and skylight on the second floor. In fact, the material concept in the context of the sustainability goals of the '2000-Watt Society' formulated for the city of Zurich corresponds to our philosophy of an expedient economy of means. The thermally activated load-bearing walls and ceilings, which are made of recycled concrete and are left visible, essentially define the interior atmosphere. Only a handful of other material applications complement the material canon, which is geared towards immediacy and haptic experience, and which thereby continues our urban and architectural concept of 'clear simplicity'. The omnipresent exposed concrete is complementary contrasted with acoustically effective wall cladding made of untreated round brass bars, solid oak floor boards for the exhibition spaces, and a marble floor for all public areas, which has been taken from the existing Moser building. Unlike the exhibition spaces for the Modernist Collection and the areas designated for temporary exhibitions, which have a more restrained atmosphere, the thinly applied and colour-contrasting mineral plaster surfaces in the rooms of the Emil Bührle Collection on the second floor expand the atmospheric experience. Together with a door-high spatial horizon set in brass, this primarily meets the need for intimacy of the small-format Impressionist artworks exhibited there.

Our ambition is to ensure that the extension of the Kunsthaus Zürich will be perceived as a natural part of the city, and only time will tell whether or not we succeeded. It is not for us architects to feel this resonance, whether in appreciation or rejection, but rather for the residents and visitors of the city of Zurich.

—
View from the south
over Heimplatz

View from the south-east   Main entrance on Heimplatz

View from the south-west

Heimplatz facade (view from the south)

—
View from the east towards
the Moser building

—
View from the north-west

Facade detail

Following page:
Facade towards garden
(north elevation)

Hall, museum shop entrance

Cash desk and information

—
Ballroom entrance,
ground floor

Staircase hall to the passage

Following page:
Ballroom

FOYER WALTER HAEFNER

—
Central hall,
view to the north

—
Staircase hall,
transition to garden

Staircase hall

View into collection gallery

Collection galleries, first floor

Exhibition gallery, second floor

Collection galleries, second floor

Collection gallery, second floor

Site plan

↑ N
100 m

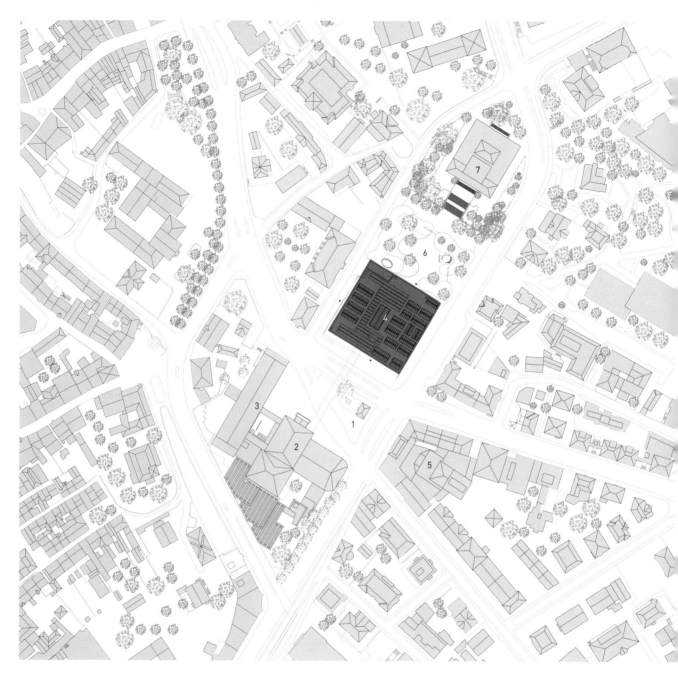

Site plan

↑ N
50 m

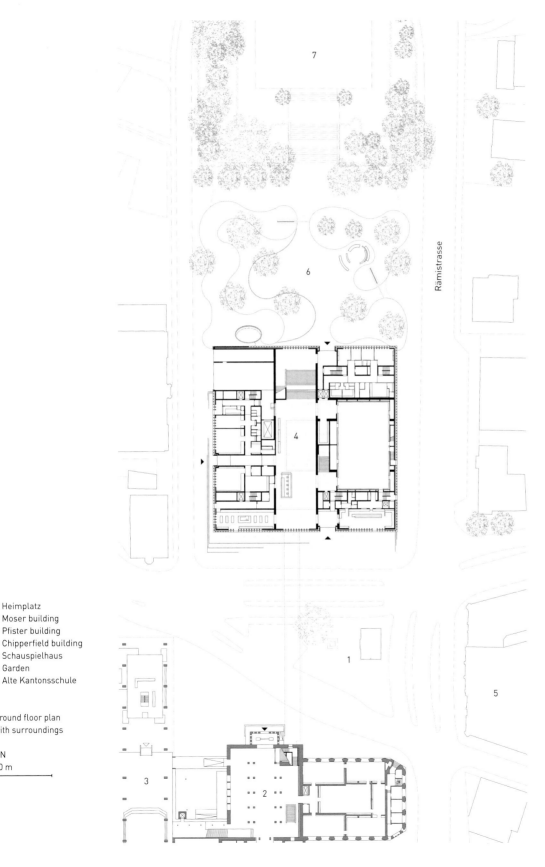

Rämistrasse

Heimplatz
Moser building
Pfister building
Chipperfield building
Schauspielhaus
Garden
Alte Kantonsschule

Ground floor plan
with surroundings

N
0 m

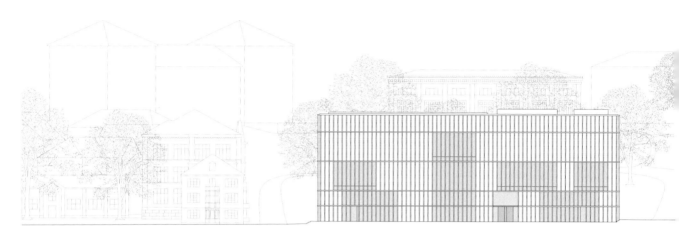

South elevation

20 m

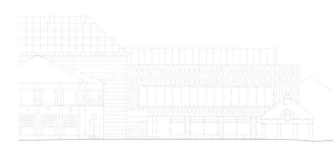

East elevation

20 m

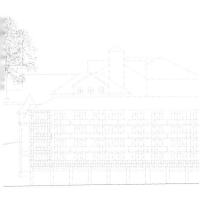

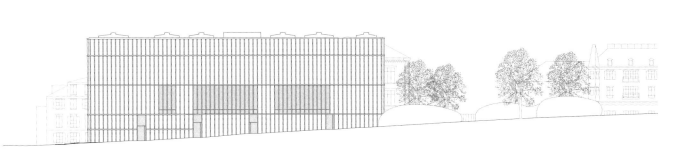

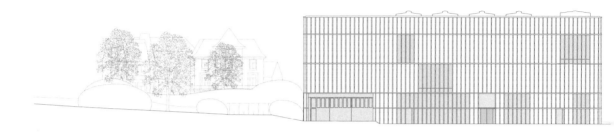

West elevation

20 m

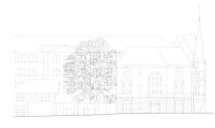

North elevation

20 m

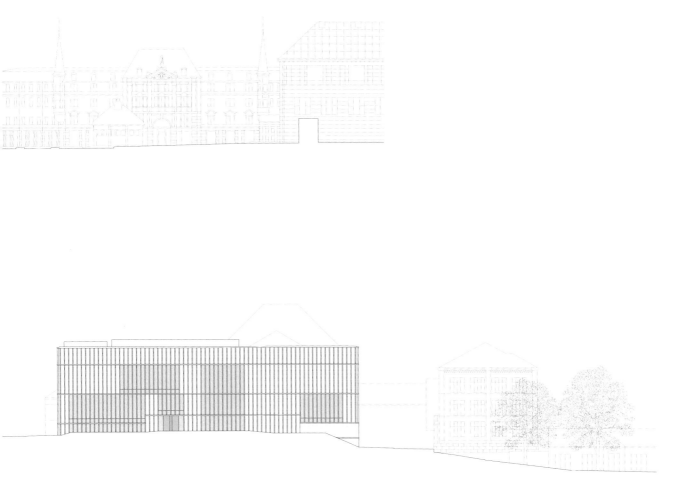

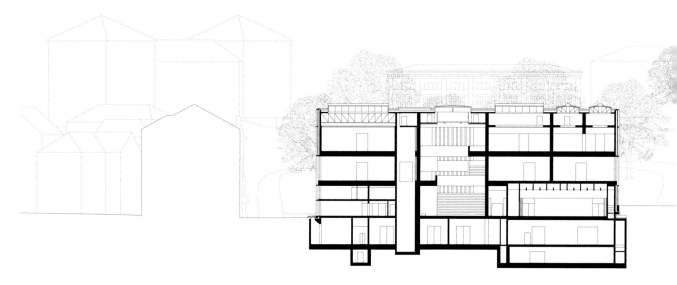

Cross section A–A

20 m

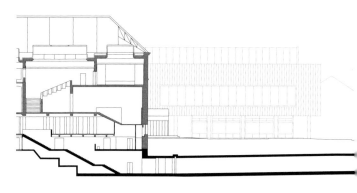

Longitudinal section B–B

20 m

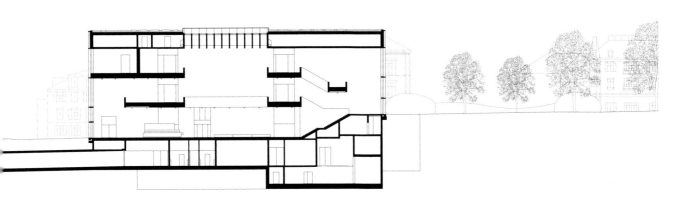

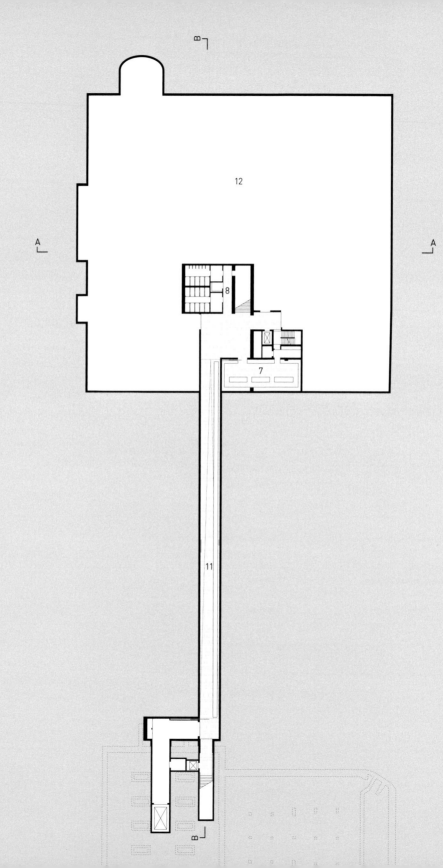

Lower ground floor plan
public area

↖N
20 m

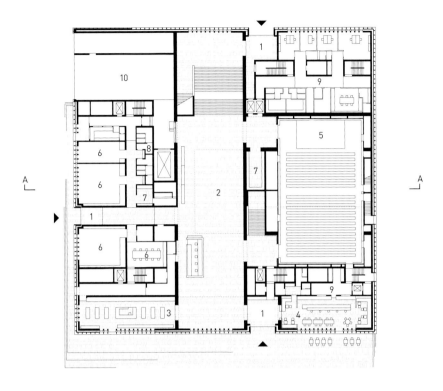

1 Entrance
2 Central hall
3 Shop
4 Café, bar
5 Ballroom
6 Art education
7 Cloakroom
8 Toilets
9 Kitchen
10 Delivery
11 Underground passage
12 Storage, workshops

Ground floor plan

N
20 m

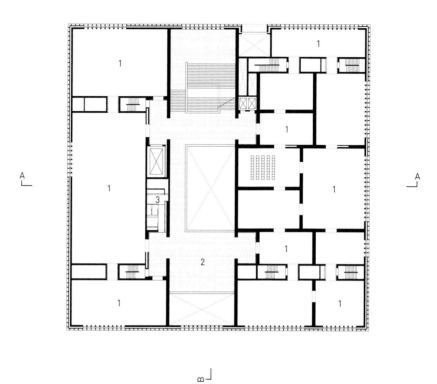

1 Collection galleries
2 Central hall
3 Toilets

First floor plan
Collection

↖N
20 m

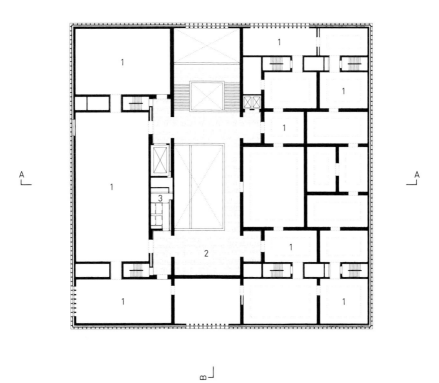

Second floor plan
Collection and exhibition

↖N
20 m

1 Natural stone facade (from outside to inside):
· rounded pilaster facade, fixed to load-bearing wall
  to prevent tilting
· core insulation, rock wool
· reinforced concrete with thermal component
  activation
· internal plastering
2 Prefabricated cast stone element
3 Pilaster in front of windows: prefabricated cast
  stone element
4 Exterior solar shading:
· vertical wind-resistant textile blinds
· motor-driven, fire-detector-controlled
· hidden guide rails behind sheet-metal lining of
  the window jambs
5 Window element:
· thermally broken aluminium window frames,
  colour-coated, circumferential, full-storey height
· frames continuously insulated, internally vapour-
  proofed, externally watertight
· sheet-metal lining of the side jambs, sun-shading
  sub-layer, foot-plate and windowsill: aluminium
  sheet, colour-coated
· clear thermally insulated triple glazing overall
  construction RC4/P6B (minus certification)
6 Interior roller blind with light-diffusing panel:
· counter-tension system (running from below to
  above), automised
· side-mounted hidden guide rails: aluminium sheet,
  colour-coated
· maintenance access via a base flap between pillars
7 Pillar, inner side:
  load-bearing, reinforced concrete, plastered
8 Supply air duct:
  air outlet through joint between wall and floor

Facade detail

1 m

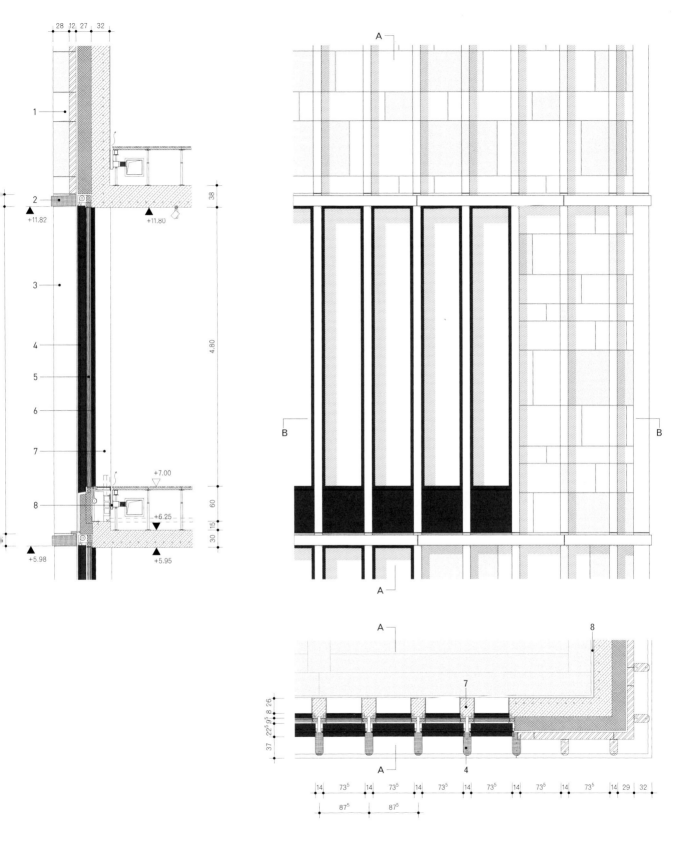

—
Heimplatz facade
(view from the south)

FACTS AND FUNCTIONS

COMPETITION
2008

PROJECT START
2009

CONSTRUCTION START
2015

COMPLETION
2020

OPENING
2021

GROSS FLOOR AREA
23 300 m²

CLIENT
Einfache Gesellschaft Kunsthaus
Erweiterung – EGKE

PROJECT MANAGEMENT
Building Surveyor's Office,
City of Zurich

OWNER
Stiftung Zürcher Kunsthaus

USER
Zürcher Kunstgesellschaft

ARCHITECT
David Chipperfield Architects
Berlin

PARTNER
David Chipperfield
Christoph Felger (Design lead)
Harald Müller

PROJECT MANAGEMENT
Hans Krause (Competition 2008)
Barbara Koller (2009–2016)
Jan Parth (2017–2021)

PROJECT TEAM

Markus Bauer
(Deputy project architect, 2009–2014)
Robert Westphal
(Deputy project architect, 2015–2020)
Wolfgang Baumeister
Leander Bulst
Beate Dauth
Kristen Finke
Pavel Frank
Anne Hengst
Ludwig Jahn
Frithjof Kahl
Guido Kappius
Jan-Philipp Neuer
Mariska Rohde
Diana Schaffrannek
Eva-Maria Stadelmann
Marc Warrington

Graphics, visualisation
Konrad Basan
Dalia Liksaite
Maude Orban
Ken Polster
Antonia Schlegel
Simon Wiesmaier
Ute Zscharnt

COMPETITION TEAM

Ivan Dimitrov
Kristen Finke
Annette Flohrschütz
Pavel Frank
Gesche Gerber
Peter von Matuschka
Sebastian von Oppen
Mariska Rohde
Franziska Rusch
Lilli Scherner
Lani Tran Duc
Marc Warrington

Graphics, visualisation
Dalia Liksaite
Antonia Schlegel
Ute Zscharnt

In collaboration with

COSTS, DATES, TENDERING
b + p baurealisation AG, Zurich

EXECUTIVE ARCHITECT
b + p baurealisation AG, Zurich
David Michel, Christian Gruober,
Lena Ackermann, Hannes Mathis

OVERALL MANAGEMENT
Niels Hochuli, Dreicon AG, Zurich

STRUCTURAL ENGINEER
IGB Ingenieurgruppe Bauen,
Karlsruhe
dsp – Ingenieure & Planer AG,
Greifensee
Ingenieurgemeinschaft
Kunsthauserweiterung, Zurich

SERVICES ENGINEER
Polke, Ziege, von Moos AG, Zurich
Hefti. Hess. Martignoni. Holding AG,
Aarau

BUILDING PHYSICS
Kopitsis Bauphysik AG, Wohlen

FIRE CONSULTANT
Gruner AG, Basel
ContiSwiss, Zurich

FACADE CONSULTANT
Emmer Pfenninger Partner AG,
Münchenstein

LIGHTING CONSULTANT
Artificial light
matí AG Lichtgestaltung, Adliswil

Daylight
Institut für Tageslichttechnik,
Stuttgart

SIGNAGE
L2M3 Kommunikationsdesign
GmbH, Stuttgart

LANDSCAPE ARCHITECT
Wirtz International nv, Schoten
KOLB Landschaftsarchitektur
GmbH, Zurich

IMPRINT

This book is being published on the occasion of the opening of the Kunsthaus Zürich's new extension building in autumn of 2021.

Realised with funds from the Einfache Gesellschaft Kunsthaus-Erweiterung (EGKE).

–

Concept and editing:
Kunsthaus Zürich,
David Chipperfield Architects Berlin
Translation and proofreading:
Gegensatz Translation Collective
Design: Büro4, Zurich
Pre-press, printing and binding:
DZA Druckerei zu Altenburg GmbH, Thuringia

–

© 2021 Einfache Gesellschaft Kunsthaus-Erweiterung, Zürcher Kunstgesellschaft / Kunsthaus Zürich and Verlag Scheidegger & Spiess AG, Zurich

–

Verlag Scheidegger & Spiess
Niederdorfstrasse 54
8001 Zurich
Switzerland
www.scheidegger-spiess.ch

–

Scheidegger & Spiess is being supported by the Federal Office of Culture with a general subsidy for the years 2021–2024.

–

ISBN 978-3-03942-027-8

German edition:
ISBN 978-3-03942-026-1

French edition:
ISBN 978-3-03942-028-5

IMAGE CREDITS

Portrait, page 6:
© Benjamin McMahon
Concept sketch, page 24:
© Christoph Felger /
David Chipperfield Architects Berlin
Portrait, page 25:
© Marion Schönenberger
for David Chipperfield Architects Berlin
Photographs, pages 30–67, 84:
© Noshe
Plans, pages 68–83:
© David Chipperfield Architects Berlin